For Isa & Ken
love and best wishes from
Jean & Bill
*

LADDEREDGE
and
COTISLEA

BIRTLEY ARIS
PETER BENNET

We thought that we were living now
but we were living then
ANNE STEVENSON

First published inGreat Britain in 2017 by
Enchiridion, 15 Connaught Gardens, Forest Hall,
Newcastle upon Tyne NE12 8AT

Designed by Michael Seal

Printed by Robsonprint, Hexham

A CIP catalogue record for this book
is available from the British Library
ISBN 978-0-9567147-3-2

LADDEREDGE AND COTISLEA

For Margaret, Michael, Anne, and Stella

Towards the farm at which I am permitted
inside the barn and then to climb the hay bales
is an old man with a scythe says Youngster
unwrapping as I skip to greet him sacking
from the blade. He slides the stone along
long time. I think I see my mother's hand
withdrawn from drawing curtains at a window
slip back into that room with the aroma
of nearly damp encyclopaedias.
Mind can touch mind. I feel my tongue
begin to press the past. The box
that sits on the table called Occasional
her fingers rest upon has mirrored drawers
whose memories are asking me to speak.
The chimney whispers to the clean cold hearth.

The brave boys that have gone away
will march back home one sunny day.

You can't get what you need for love nor money.
I do not understand how that it is
the opposite direction for the lane
will join the road towards a future farther
than Buxton is or Macclesfield and people
After the War Before the War
are selling what they do to live. It's called
the World of Work. It's in a dream
I hear them talk. I'm half awake.
What can you do? There aren't the men.
There is a doll to be undressed
and school books of my uncles who are dead
but aren't dead now of course but are Called Up
like Daddy who I don't know yet.
It seems you have an interest in silence
and oily dust where nothing is disturbed
in which case you will want to hear
about an Austin Seven up on blocks
behind its blistered garage doors
and petrol rations. There's a fox
all night in Mollock's Wood. I think he tries
to sing to me. I am asleep.

And with the big girls in the gorse
who tell things and play Truth Or Dare or worse.

Caterpillar Tractor is the best thing.
Milk Cart though comes every morning
with that horse has a name that I can say
but I don't know it now. The dippers clatter
with different voices and are big and little
to lift milk from the churn. Someone is laughing.
The same hand from the curtains holds the jug.
I paint an outhouse door with Dolly Blue
which makes it wet not blue. Another fox
I think sings like the one I know at night
up on the roof the wind turns. Later a pond
has a spit where I will dig a grave
among the tree roots where I know
it is the best place for a Viking cat.
As well in future I will have my bus fare
to where the vet lives and back with her dead.
That place will also be where Harvey
shows us his Circumcision. Up the lane
the cows come which have heavy tails.
I stalk them in my wellingtons.

Another laugh. Jam Rags on the line. A shout.
Toys in a van. Demobbed. The air is soot.

The ceiling light hangs like a chandelier
with fitments where gas mantles were
and has a middle that's a crown.
It has to go and crashes. I will try
to wear it in a cloud of dust.
Daddy is hammering. Outside air is clean.
At night I shall not hear the fox.
But in the day is Blow Lamp. Paint comes off.
Even Lincrusta. The house is old
and has a cellar but will be like new.
The curtains are not wide enough.
Hands will bring poppers that will keep them shut
and rise to stitch against the sun.
The house is in a marl field. That means clay.
And where the pond is it is like a lake.
The Viking sea. I have a Siren Suit
and talk to grown-up children at the gate
when street lights being lit. I think I've come
a long way off and they don't like my name.

*It's nearly Christmas what it is. I wake
in time for Daddy's Home Now motorbike.*

The bully has a needle with a hilt
like a sword. It is a hat pin.
He is the torturer outside the outside
lavatory. He shall stay where air is soot.
I'll make a notice for a Zoo and tie it
big to the garden gate. No one will come.
There's just the goldfish and the toad
that's always in the coal-shed but today
is not. I do not know what's true when that is
but you will know by now. We're on a Walk.
Mummy that's the hands and Daddy
and pushchair Margaret. I find butter
in fresh packets hid behind a tree beside
the path where no one lives. It is Black Market
so we will take it home and not
Waste Time Worrying. Another day
we hear a voice that shouts A Murrain On Ye
at us from a bleak barn with an echo.

Christmas occurs and Santa Claus
and tears and frightening said and slamming doors.

There is a worse dream or maybe a part
that happens on its own and seems
more anxious. There are lavatories again
but this time made by sculptors out of junk
like driftwood with some paint adhering, toys
and car parts and with various containers.
Some are stuck up in the air and shaky
and some are squelchy underground.
The creatures that are queueing see right in.
They don't know me. Though some are nice
most are indifferent and grunt
or if they seem like women they will sigh.
I should have something that I do to sell
but all I've got is words they grab
and look at upside down. It is the World
of Work. They cannot read but like to feel
the paper. Martin lives in a Council House.
His Dad has a shed with tools. One day he lets
us have a log and hammers and a bag
of panel pins. We knock them in
and trying not to bend them till the log
is heavy Heaven with a thousand stars.

You only need to blink to think
about me and the years between us shrink.

The Tip is where we go along the track
out into fields by Whittle's shop.
You smell it burning and not breathing parts
are sticky hot. That's where we find what treasure
is to play with. There are gas masks and helmets
and sometimes German ones and bayonets
and bicycles to put together bits.
There's a story that's got me in it before
all that which Mummy tells she laughs about.
Perhaps you'll laugh as well for listening.
The Combine Harvester has stopped
and waits and tucks its shadow in. It's time
for sandwiches and lemonade
but there are men with guns around the island
that is still standing crop. I hear the rustle
of the rabbits very frightened and the hares
as well there with me and the shot-gun barrels
click into place. What happens is
that my red hat and me are glimpsed
in one small movement of the corn.
The guns are lowered and the air is heavy
and by my movement and because that moment
I shall live as long as you exactly.
Mummy what are you thinking of
or chatting to a Land Girl without thought?
There is another Walk and when it's frosty
so Magic Lane is pink because the sky
and there are clouds shaped like a T
because it's Time for Tea which Daddy says.
I race him home. He lets me win.

Who has a mo-mo off the Tip?
Whose little mo-mo says Pip Pip?

Up the road I must not where are different
children is a pumping station
abandoned with a bashed-in door
with old machinery and rust
and knee deep water trouble happens with.
The different children Mummy says are Rough.
This summer there is hidden grass
between the clumps of gorse up at the top
of Back Field where the big girls are
that show their knickers. It's tea-time again
but late and Daddy in the distance looking.
Uncle George is not my uncle
but Mr Gibson who makes cider
drip through straw that smell I like.
One day I shall say odoriferous
and sesquipedalian for you too.
He saws a Walking Stick be short for me.
Now when the sun keeps still I go
down in the big weeds living in his garden
to where it's warming at a wall where once
upon a time he tied an Animal.
It has an iron ring that hangs
to put my nose in that's still low enough
for me wherever it has gone to now.

Pig in the book has nose that has a ring
so ring has nose will be a funny thing.

But in another dream my head slides through
and then I see it. I am on my own
more frightened now than ever I remember
and footsteps on the landing in the night
until I pay attention. What I say
even in the sun that's in the garden
or in the wood where foxes sing
goes to a dark mask in a circular
hat shape that's huge and is an ear as well
and like the inside of a black umbrella.
But it will also go to you-that's-me -
an old man in an armchair looking back.
The other fox does not turn in the wind
above my bed but on a different roof
on Woodside Lane one day he winks
when Mummy Look At Fox and lifts me up.
The work that is the world is time.

Daddy will crank my bed into a car.
I drive to sleep. He did not like the War.

Down the road there is a Bottling Machine
and Sour that is the bad smell. Mr Clayton
brings milk with a Milk Float now and has no horse
but Ferrets that want all the time to eat
my fingers. I'm putting off the worst thing.
This summer too is time for Dens
in Coppice Wood and Mollock's Wood to hide
and hunt and find the others first.
I have forgotten home is where-am-I
once more when Daddy worried so of course
it's not the first occasion or the last
and it is not the worst thing which is what
it is that only happens once for ever.

In due course we shall come to that.
Biffs to the head will cause imagination.
But Mummy says I worry him too much
about me that I'll worry him to death.

I've watched my father reach for breath and die.
I'm reading Biggles. Boys don't cry.

I see the place he used to hang
his leather Crash Hat and his Goggles
are hidden somewhere what I think
and Gauntlets gone were on the kitchen chair.
But may I still go out to play?
September's coming and with engines chewing
fog and steam and smoke and fire and hauling
vacant carriages with sepia photographs
and luggage racks like fishing nets and me
along the soon closed Churnet Valley Line
to stop at Rudyard Lake, Cliffe Park and Rushton,
Bosley Halt, North Rode, and Macclesfield.
And School. But that is always afterwards.
There's also in this summer time for jousting
on bikes with six foot garden canes
from Firth's the shop for everything.
The aim is not to stick an eye
and that could happen but to get the lance
between the spokes and throw him off.
We all have proper shields not dustbin lids
and helmets from the Tip to beat each other
with heavy sticks. It is the Middle Ages
and violent and innocent.

But there is Keith from Sunday School
too old for us who comes to show us fireworks
kept back from Bonfire Night and mice
and frogs blown up and what he does
to insects that have wings and legs.
He has a girlfriend too and tells us what
she does that's what he makes her do.
On a lawn by Woodside Lane a mower leaves
the smell that is the panic of the grass.

I think you think that what I say is Now
which means that I am nearly you.

I'm down among the dreams again and dreaming
about the big black hat that is the ear
of sleep and voices that I love the most
go silent there for ever and inside it -
Greased Lightning gone as quick as that -
and also of the mirror box
that falls from the table called Occasional
and shatters me awake. Footsteps come and hands
at night in August half-light by the marl field.
It doesn't really break. My face looks back
at me-that's-you from every drawer
but something is that sort happening she says
and pulls beside herself and me to Daddy.
We are too proud to have The Telephone
and can't afford it anyway
so she has gone to rouse them at the Dairy
but I can watch him and I always shall
where it is almost dawn and hear him breathe
like slow strokes of the stone along
long time and loud then sudden louder stop.
The scythe is sharp and I think Good.

I sold the world a life for time to do
this work for nothing, finding words for True.

Other books and pamphlets by Peter Bennet

First Impressions, with Rosemary Scott and Dave Stagg (Mandeville Press)
Sky-riding (Peterloo Poets)
The Border Hunt (Jackson's Arm)
A Clee Sequence (Lincolnshire and Humberside Arts)
All the Real (Flambard Press)
The Long Pack (Flambard Press)
Ha-Ha (Smith/Doorstop)
Noctua (Shoestring Press)
Goblin Lawn: New and Selected Poems (Flambard Press)
The Glass Swarm (Flambard Press)
Bobby Bendick's Ride, with drawings by Birtley Aris (Enchiridion)
The Game of Bear (Flambard Press)
Border (Bloodaxe Books)
Arcana, with drawings by Birtley Aris (Red Squirrel Press)

Much of Birtley Aris's work is based on poetry. In the 1970s and 1980s he designed poetry posters for the Mid Northumberland Arts Group, and produced a large number of drawings related to Edward Thomas's verse. Collaborations with contemporary poets include Acknowledged Land, 1994, Another Wild, 2004 with Linda France, and Night Train, 2009 with Sean O'Brien. Previous collaborations with Peter Bennet are Bobby Bendick's Ride, 2000, and Arcana, 2014.

Peter Bennet's poetry is known for its verbal panache, bold imaginative strokes, subversive connections and dark wit. In this uncharacteristically autobiographical and revealing poem he revisits memories from between his war-time early childhood and the age of eleven. He was born at Ladderedge, near Leek, Staffordshire. Cotislea is the name of a house his family lived in later, in Poynton, in Cheshire.